PRESENTS

RACCOON'S BAD WEEK

©2019 ALL CHARACTERS, APPEARANING IN
"THE BIG ROCK PRESENTS RACCOON'S BAD WEEK" ARE PROPERTY OF LEO GERALD BROPHY.
ANY REPRODUCTION NEEDS TO HAVE WRITTEN CONSENT OF THE AUTHOR/ARTIST.

NOW IN FULL COLOUR!

SOMETIMES A BAD ATTITUDE CAN END UP RUINING YOUR WHOLE DAY. RACCOON MAY HAVE MOUTHED OFF TO THE WRONG PERSON THIS TIME AND WHEN THE GANG ARE ALL GOING SWIMMING TOGETHER IN THEIR FAVOURITE SPOT. RACCOON'S DAY GOES FROM GREAT TO BAD.

PERHAPS HIS HAPPY DISPOSITION CAN SAVE THE DAY FOR EVERYONE AS THEY ALL GET PULLED IN FOR THE RIDE. MAKE THE BEST OF THE SITUATION AND HAVE FUN IS ALWAYS HIS MOTTO.

A COLLECTION OF COLOUR COMIC STRIPS FEATURING ROB RACCOON, SIMON SALAMANDER, MOLLY CAT, CHRONE ALLIGATOR, BOB BEAR, ALOYSIUS SNAKE, LITERAL CAT, LEO CAT, P.C. PIG, CONSERVATIVE TURTLE, POMPAS DONKEY, HUGH DIRTY RAT, MONKEY DOO, ROADKILL SQUIRELL, MADAME OCTOBER AND SMOKED SALMON.

VOLUME 3 COMING SOON...

L. BROPHY
JULY 4TH, 2019

FOR MORE INFO ON UPCOMING BOOKS AND PROJECTS FROM LEO GERALD BROPHY PLEASE VISIT:

WWW.ERISCREATIONS.COM

CHECK OUT MORE BOOKS ON AMAZON FROM THIS AUTHOR

PIGGY HOCKEY
PIGGY AND THE BIGGEST ROCK
THE BIG ROCK

ROB RACCOON, SIMON SALAMANDER, MOLLY CAT, CHRONE ALLIGATOR, BOB BEAR, ALOYSIUS SNAKE, LITERAL CAT, LEO CAT, P.C. PIG, CONSERVATIVE TURTLE, POMPAS DONKEY, HUGH DIRTY RAT, MONKEY DOO, ROADKILL SQUIRELL, MADAME OCTOBER, SMOKED SALMON ARE COPYRIGHT (2019) LEO GERALD BROPHY. THEY CANNOT BE REPRODUCED WITHOUT EXPRESS WRITTEN CONSENT OF LEO GERALD BROPHY.

THE BIG ROCK

PRESENTS

RACCOON'S BAD WEEK

www.ingramcontent.com/pod-product-compliance
Lightning Source LLC
Chambersburg PA
CBHW060502010526

44118CB00018B/2505